FOLENS IDEAS BANK INFORMATION AND LIBRARY SKILLS

Richard Brown

Contents

How to use this book	2	Types of text 3	26
Introduction	3	Making and using a glossary	28
Alphabetical lists	4	Finding the main idea 1	30
The Dewey Decimal System 1	6	Finding the main idea 2	32
The Dewey Decimal System 2	8	Comparing texts on the same subject	34
The Dewey Decimal System 3	10	Facts and opinions	36
What helps you find the book you want?	12	The language of persuasion	38
Using a contents page	14	Information to persuade	40
Using an index	16	Using the question and answer form	42
How information is organised on the page	18	Ways of presenting information	44
Formulating key questions	20	What I thought about my project	46
Types of text 1	22	Eight ways to help ...	48
Types of text 2	24		

Folens Publishers

How to use this book

Ideas Bank books provide you with ready to use, practical photocopiable activity pages for children **plus** a wealth of ideas for extension and development.

TEACHER IDEAS PAGE — PHOTOCOPIABLE ACTIVITY PAGE

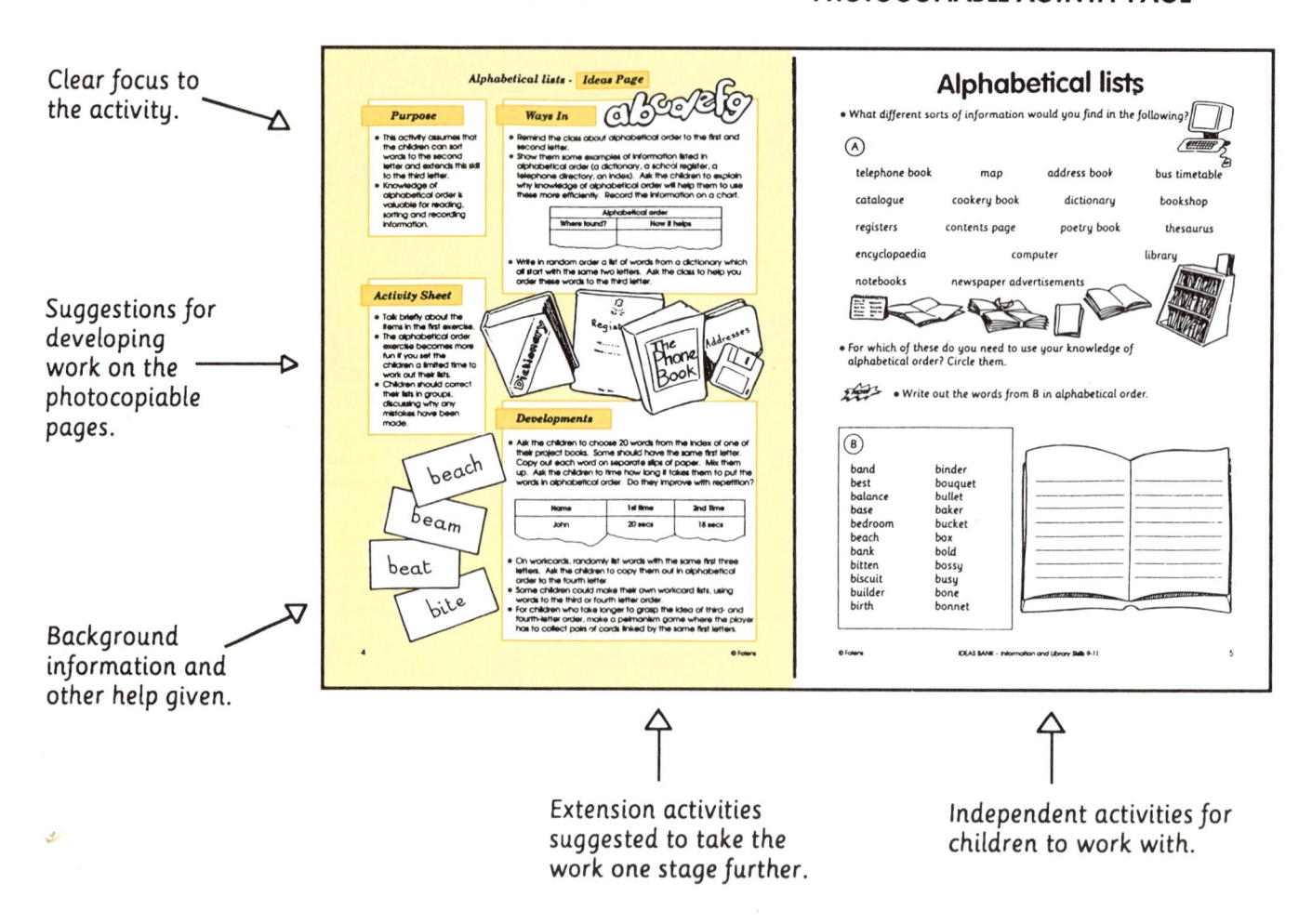

Clear focus to the activity.

Suggestions for developing work on the photocopiable pages.

Background information and other help given.

Extension activities suggested to take the work one stage further.

Independent activities for children to work with.

- Time saving, relevant and practical, **Ideas Bank** books ensure that you will always have work ready at hand.

Folens books are protected by international copyright laws. All rights reserved. The copyright of all materials in this book, except where otherwise stated, remains the property of the publisher and author(s). No part of this publication may be reproduced, stored in a retrieval system, or transmitted, in any form or by any means, for whatever purpose, without the written permission of Folens Limited.

Folens do allow photocopying of selected pages of this publication for educational use, providing that this use is within the confines of the purchasing institution. You may make as many copies as you require for classroom.

This resource may be used in a variety of ways; however, it is not intended that teachers or students should write into the book itself.
The author and publisher would like to thank the following for permission to reproduce material:
Watts Books for *Timelines: Flight, Fliers and Flying Machines* by David Jeffries (1991); page 15.
Dorling Kindersley for *Amazing Boats* by Margarette Lincoln (1992); page 17.

Richard Brown hereby asserts his moral right to be identified as the author of this work in accordance with the Copyright, Designs and Patents Act 1988. © 1994 Folens Limited, on behalf of the author.

Cover by: In Touch Creative Services Ltd.   Illustrations by: Rob Chapman.   Cover illustration: Valeria Petrone.
First published 1994 by Folens Limited, Albert House, Apex Business Centre, Boscombe Road, Dunstable, LU5 4RL, England.
ISBN 185276795-2   Printed in Singapore by Craft Print.

Introduction

In their first years of school, children learn to read through stories and rhymes. The information books they encounter during this time are mainly pictorial, narrative in form and personal in tone.

By contrast, the information books they are expected to read once they have achieved a degree of fluency and independence in reading are often non-narrative in style, require a wide range of reading skills, contain much that assumes a prior knowledge of the subject, and use diagrams, tables, charts, maps, alphabetical lists, timelines and other devices alongside pictures and text.

Learning to read through fiction and poetry in isolation is not an adequate preparation for coping with information texts. In the early stages, children need to learn a range of other reading and information retrieval skills. These include:
- looking at the difference between literature and information texts
- gaining information from the book's cover and pictures
- examining the ways information books present and organise information
- understanding classification
- identifying alphabetical order to the second letter
- using contents and index pages
- posing key questions for research
- reading for relevance
- labelling
- note-taking using underlining
- looking at chronological texts
- developing a personal view of project work.

The activities in this book help children to develop an understanding of these areas and build on this foundation.

The organisation of the material

This book has 22 activities, each accompanied by a resource page, which is divided into four parts:
Purpose: this gives the activity's underlying rationale. It shows the reasons for teaching it and which reading and information retrieval skills can be developed through it.
Ways In: this suggests a way to introduce and carry out the activity.

Activity Sheet: this is an integral part of the sequence set out in the *Ways In* section. Most activities are introductory, so it makes sense to link the skills taught through them directly to the class project. Such links are important if the activities are to have useful and lasting value for each child.
Developments: this section presents ideas for extending the activity, as group work, classroom displays or the creation of resources. The ideas will also be useful for those children who may need more work than that afforded by the activity sheet.

A subject-based guide to the activities:

Subject	Page
Acid rain	23
Aeroplanes	15
Alphabets	5
Boats	17
Book design	19, 43
Britain today	37
Cars	23, 41
Castles	31
Catalogue cards	13
Fire	33
Fuel	23
Holidays	39
Pollution	23, 41
Queen Victoria	27
Rainfall	25, 29
Seashore	43
Van Gogh	35
Weather	25, 29

Alphabetical lists - Ideas Page

Purpose

- This activity assumes that the children can sort words to the second letter and extends this skill to the third letter.
- Knowledge of alphabetical order is valuable for reading, sorting and recording information.

Ways In

- Remind the class about alphabetical order to the first and second letter.
- Show them some examples of information listed in alphabetical order (a dictionary, a school register, a telephone directory, an index). Ask the children to explain why knowledge of alphabetical order will help them to use these more efficiently. Record the information on a chart.

Alphabetical order	
Where found?	How it helps

- Write in random order a list of words from a dictionary which all start with the same two letters. Ask the class to help you order these words to the third letter.

Activity Sheet

- Talk briefly about the items in the first exercise.
- The alphabetical order exercise becomes more fun if you set the children a limited time to work out their lists.
- Children should correct their lists in groups, discussing why any mistakes have been made.

Developments

- Ask the children to choose 20 words from the index of one of their project books. Some should have the same first letter. Copy out each word on separate slips of paper. Mix them up. Ask the children to time how long it takes them to put the words in alphabetical order. Do they improve with repetition?

Name	1st time	2nd Time
John	20 secs	18 secs

- On workcards, randomly list words with the same first three letters. Ask the children to copy them out in alphabetical order to the fourth letter.
- Some children could make their own workcard lists, using words to the third or fourth letter order.
- For children who take longer to grasp the idea of third- and fourth-letter order, make a pelmanism game where the player has to collect pairs of cards linked by the same first letters.

4

© Folens

Alphabetical lists

- What different sorts of information would you find in the following?

A

telephone book	map	address book	bus timetable
catalogue	cookery book	dictionary	bookshop
registers	contents page	poetry book	thesaurus
encyclopaedia		computer	library
notebooks	newspaper advertisements		

- For which of these do you need to use your knowledge of alphabetical order? Circle them.

NOW • Write out the words from B in alphabetical order.

B

band	binder
best	bouquet
balance	bullet
base	baker
bedroom	bucket
beach	box
bank	bold
bitten	bossy
biscuit	busy
builder	bone
birth	bonnet

The Dewey Decimal System 1 - Ideas Page

Purpose

- Public libraries and most school libraries use the standard Dewey Decimal System to classify their books.
- This and the following two activities introduce the main Dewey subject classifications and their corresponding Dewey numbers. They give the children practice in this library skill.
- These activities are only possible if children have access to books which are ordered using the Dewey Decimal System.

Ways In

- If possible, carry out this activity in the school library where the books are clearly shelved and numbered according to the Dewey System. Failing this, collect books for each subject classification, making sure they have their numbers attached.
- Explain the universal nature of the Dewey system, and how learning to use it is an essential skill for library users.
- Information books are grouped into ten very broad subjects. Each book in these ten subjects is given a number called a Dewey number. The system was named after Melvil Dewey (1851–1931), an American librarian. Section 8, Literature, has been omitted because of its broad nature.

Activity Sheet

- If you have a subject index in the library, refer to it to show the range of subjects within each category and to demonstrate how it can be used as a reference.
- Explain that each category has its own range of numbers. Children could suggest why this is necessary. Discuss the subheadings in each Dewey box.
- Ask the children which shelf they would go to if they were looking for information about: machines, Easter, famous people, water, Vikings. Point out that they may have to look in more than one category, because subjects overlap.
- To enable the activity to run smoothly, divide the class into groups of three or four. Give each group a different starting point: group 1 starts at 0, and group 2 starts at 300.

Developments

- Revise the work in the library a few days later to remind the children of the system.
- If possible, take the class to the local library with a new set of activity sheets and carry out the same exercise.
- Ask the children to concentrate on section 8. Why was it not included on their activity sheet? What kinds of books would be found? The list should be seen to be enormous. Ask them to find examples from poetry, novels and Shakespeare.

MACHINES 621.8, 610.28, 614.838
WATER 553.7, 333.91, 628.1
EASTER 372.19, 783.65, 232, 745.5941
FAMOUS PEOPLE 920.02
VIKINGS 948.02, 293.13, 942.01

Section 8
Literature and Poetry

Reasons why this section was not included:

1. There are too many books in this section.

Section 8
Literature and Poetry

What I found on the library shelves:

Novels
Anthologies
Story books
Shakespeare plays
Drama

© Folens

The Dewey System

- Find a book for each category. Write in the title and Dewey number.

0–99 General

eg newspapers
encyclopaedias
museums

Title:
Number:

100–199.9 The Mind (philosophy)

eg thinking
dreams
ideas

Title:
Number:

200–299.9 Religion

eg Islam
The Bible
Saints
Buddhism

Title:
Number:

300–399.9 Social Sciences

eg the environment
families
cities
law
education
lifeboats
money

Title:
Number:

400–499.9 Language

eg alphabets
English language

Title:
Number:

500–599.9 Science

eg maths
astronomy
time
light and heat
plants
pre-history

Title:
Number:

600–699.9 Technology

eg the body and health
engineering
farming
cooking
shops
trade

Title:
Number:

700–799.9 Art, Sport and Recreation

eg architecture
crafts
photography
athletics
music

Title:
Number:

900–999.9 Geography, History and Biography

eg atlases
famous people
ancient world
Europe
Asia, Africa, Americas

Title:
Number:

© Folens   IDEAS BANK – Information and Library Skills   7

The Dewey Decimal System 2 - Ideas Page

Purpose

- Children usually approach a library with a specific enquiry in mind. Their first question should be: 'In which section should I look for books on this subject?'
- To answer this, the child has to be able to classify the subject within one of the ten Dewey categories. For example, a book on bats would be in the Science section (599); a book on puppets in the Arts section (791).
- Such classification is often neither obvious nor straightforward, and more than one Dewey heading might apply; so practice in this library work is required.

Ways In

- If possible, carry out this activity in the school library, where you can refer to the way the bookshelves are organised.
- Remind the children of the Dewey Decimal System and how it works.
- Hold up some information books and ask the children where they should be shelved in the library.

Activity Sheet

- For the purpose of this exercise, most of the numbers after the decimal point have been ignored. Let the children use them if you wish and then explain how these numbers create finer categorisations within a subject.

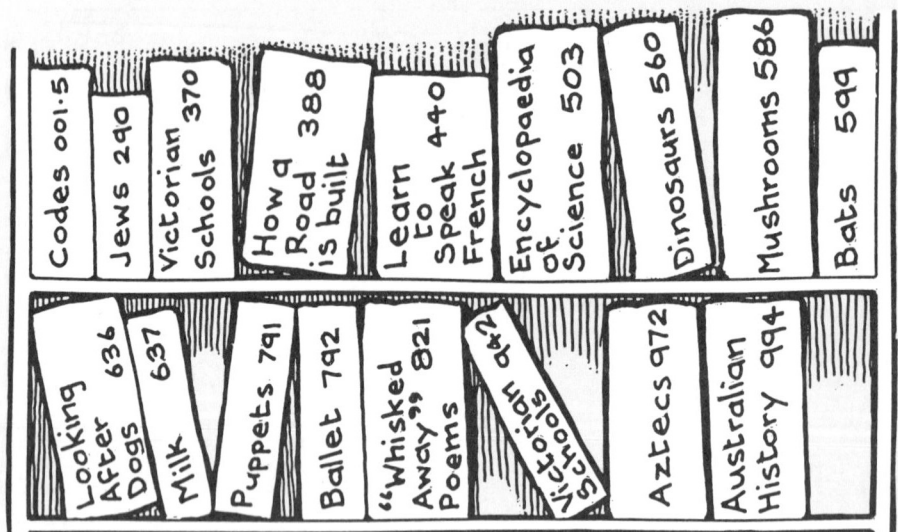

A plan of our library

Developments

- Ask the children to draw a plan of how the shelves are organised in the school library. This makes the link between the work of this activity sheet and their own library more obvious. They could also draw books for each shelf, perhaps testing each other using real books with the Dewey number temporarily covered.
- For those who need further work with the Dewey numbers, make a list of titles on a sheet and assign each one two Dewey numbers, one correct and one incorrect. The child should cross out the incorrect numbers by referring to the numbers of the ten Dewey sections in the school library (or on the activity sheets already used).
- Organise a rota of library monitors to reshelve used library books in the correct place, using the Dewey numbers.

© Folens

Library shelves

- Read the titles of these books.

Bats | Australian History | Ballet | Aztecs | Looking After Dogs | Victorian Schools | Codes | Learn to Speak French | Jews | "Whisked Away" Poems | How a Road is Built | Dinosaurs | Puppets | Encyclopaedia of Science | Mushrooms | Milk

- Discuss where they should go on the shelves and then draw the books in the correct places.

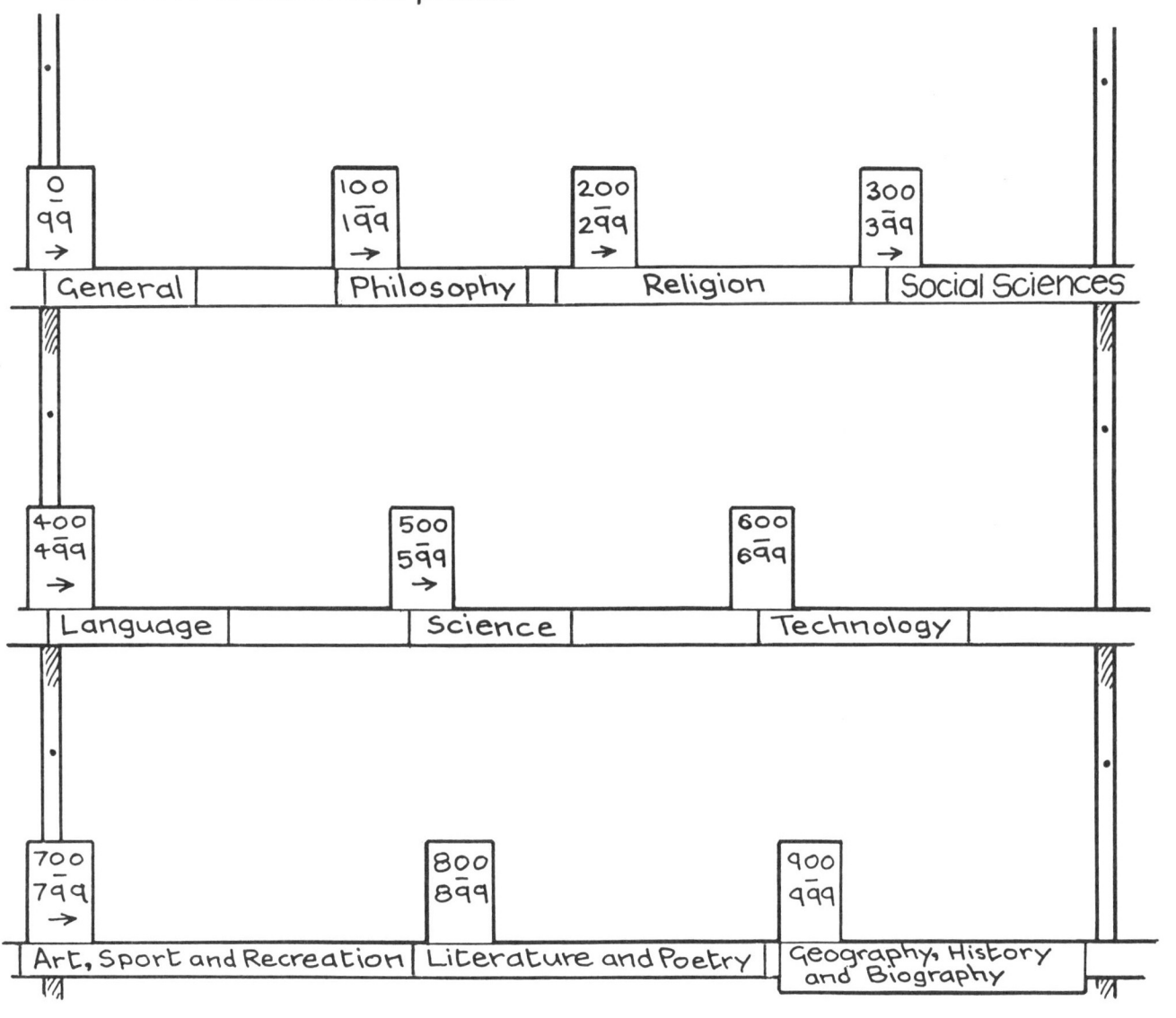

Shelf 1:
- 0–99 → General
- 100–199 → Philosophy
- 200–299 → Religion
- 300–399 → Social Sciences

Shelf 2:
- 400–499 → Language
- 500–599 → Science
- 600–699 → Technology

Shelf 3:
- 700–799 → Art, Sport and Recreation
- 800–899 → Literature and Poetry
- 900–999 → Geography, History and Biography

© Folens   IDEAS BANK – *Information and Library Skills*

The Dewey Decimal System 3 - Ideas Page

Purpose

- This activity links typical questions that children might ask to those Dewey categories that are most likely to provide the answers.
- The activity encourages children to approach library work with clear questions in mind.
- It helps them to classify their enquiry, to make their search for the correct book more efficient and successful.
- It encourages the children to learn the ten Dewey categories by heart.

Ways In

- Remind the children of the Dewey system and how it works.

Category	Number
General	0–99
Philosophy	100–199
Religion	200–299
Social Sciences	300–399
Language	400–499
Science	500–599
Technology	600–699
Art, Sport and Recreation	700–799
Literature and Poetry	800–899
Geography, History and Biography	900–999

- Talk to the children about the usefulness of learning the ten Dewey categories by heart and then discuss different ways of making the learning easier. For example, some children may find it easier to learn the initials of each category as a sequence first, G-P-R-S-L-S-T-A-L-G, perhaps counting on their fingers. Others might like to invent mnemonics.

Where do diamonds come from? 400 - 499.9

What are satellites for? 600 - 699.9

What do Hindus believe? 200 - 299.9

How do you make ice-cream? 700 - 799.9

Where is Mount Kilimanjaro? 900 - 999.9

Activity Sheet

- The categories and numbers for each question should be fairly obvious to the children, but some may want to use the school library to help them find the answers and this should be encouraged.
- Do not allow children to use the General category for any of the answers, although in any real enquiry recourse to encyclopaedias may be the quickest route to an answer.
- Check the answers together as a class at the end. In doing so, point out that other categories might also provide information, for example the question on Viking clothes might also be answered by reference to a book on clothes or costumes (646).

Developments

- Encourage the children to write speech bubble questions for a particular project. Copy some of these on to large speech bubbles for a display. Underneath, provide books which could supply the answers to the questions. Small groups could report back to the class.
- Display some of the activity sheets in the school library, to help other children make sense of the Dewey Decimal System.

Finding the answers

- Underneath the questions, write the Dewey categories and the numbers of the books that might provide an answer.

What did Vikings wear?

Category: History
No: 900-999

What are satellites for?

Cat: _____
No: _____

Which birds live in the Antarctic?

Cat: _____
No: _____

How do telephones work?

Cat: _____
No: _____

What did the first written language look like?

Cat: _____
No: _____

How is a road built?

Cat: _____
No: _____

Was Van Gogh French or Dutch?

Cat: _____
No: _____

Where is Mount Kilimanjaro?

Cat: _____
No: _____

What is the story in Shakespeare's Macbeth?

Cat: _____
No: _____

How do you make ice-cream?

Cat: _____
No: _____

Where do diamonds come from?

Cat: _____
No: _____

What do Hindus believe?

Cat: _____
No: _____

© Folens — IDEAS BANK – *Information and Library Skills*

What helps you find a book you want? - Ideas Page

Purpose

- This activity teaches children to locate particular titles, works by authors or books on a specific subject.
- There may be three sources of information available in a library: catalogue cards, computers or microfiches. Most public libraries have the latter two. This activity introduces children to card indexes.
- It is likely that schools will continue to use catalogue cards for some time. The aim of this activity, therefore, is to help children use catalogue cards successfully as part of their book search. It is best carried out in small groups in the library.

Ways In

- Explain how computers and microfiches can help them to find titles on a subject, books by an author or full details of one particular book. If the children have had experience of using either source in their local library, ask them to describe what they did.
- Show the children catalogue cards for a work of fiction: one for the title, one for the author.
- Show the class a subject index card and a classified index card. Ask pairs of children to note and explain the differences between them.

| Differences we noticed ||
Subject index	Classified index

Activity Sheet

- Choose up to six children to carry out the activity in the library. Make sure that at least a parent or helper is there to supervise them and perhaps to help in their searches.
- Half the group could work with the subject index first, taking it in turns to find the Dewey numbers. The other half could start with the classified index, taking it in turns to find at least one title for each subject.
- After they have reported back, children should check their answers using the school's subject index booklet or cards.

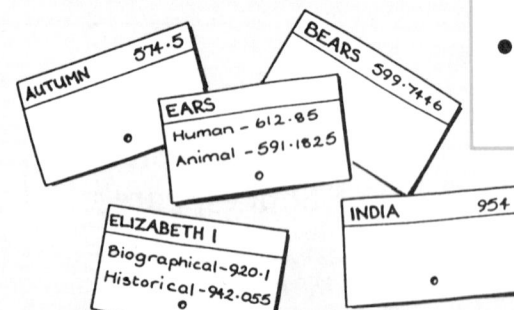

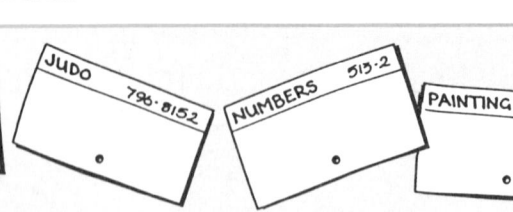

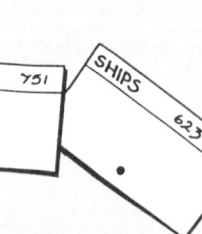

Developments

- If you feel the children need more practice in using the reference cards, ask the subject-index group to create exercises for the other group based on their activity and vice versa.
- Whenever the children are using the library to search for information, remind them to make use of the reference cards.
- Enlist their help to find books on particular subjects for a project, or by particular authors for a display.
- If the children have made project books, ask them to make a number of subject index catalogue cards for them, and one classified index card.

Finding your book

- Look at these catalogue cards.

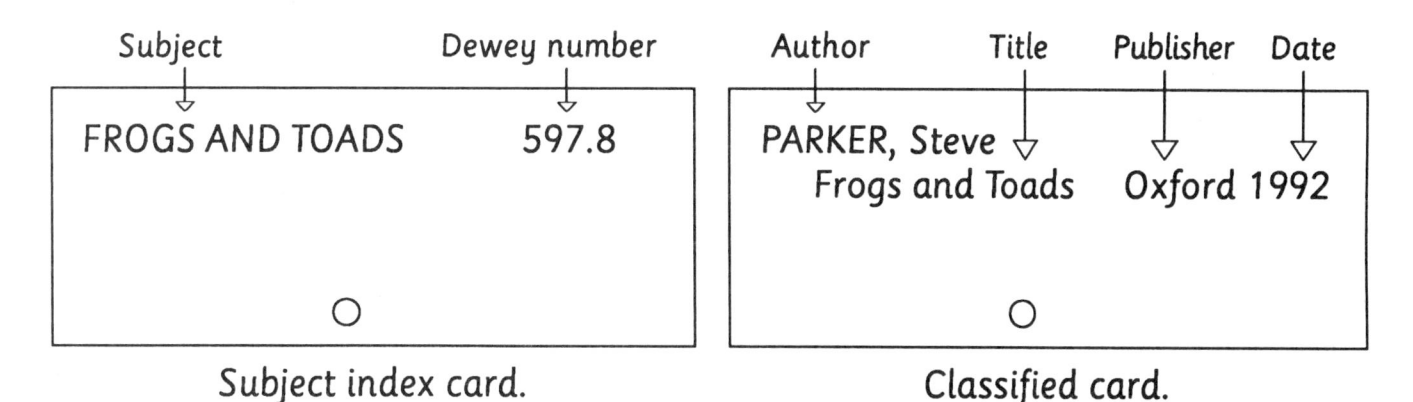

Subject → FROGS AND TOADS   Dewey number → 597.8

Subject index card.

Author → PARKER, Steve   Title → Frogs and Toads   Publisher → Oxford   Date → 1992

Classified card.

- Look in your school's subject index for the topics on the cards below.
- Write down the Dewey numbers on the cards.

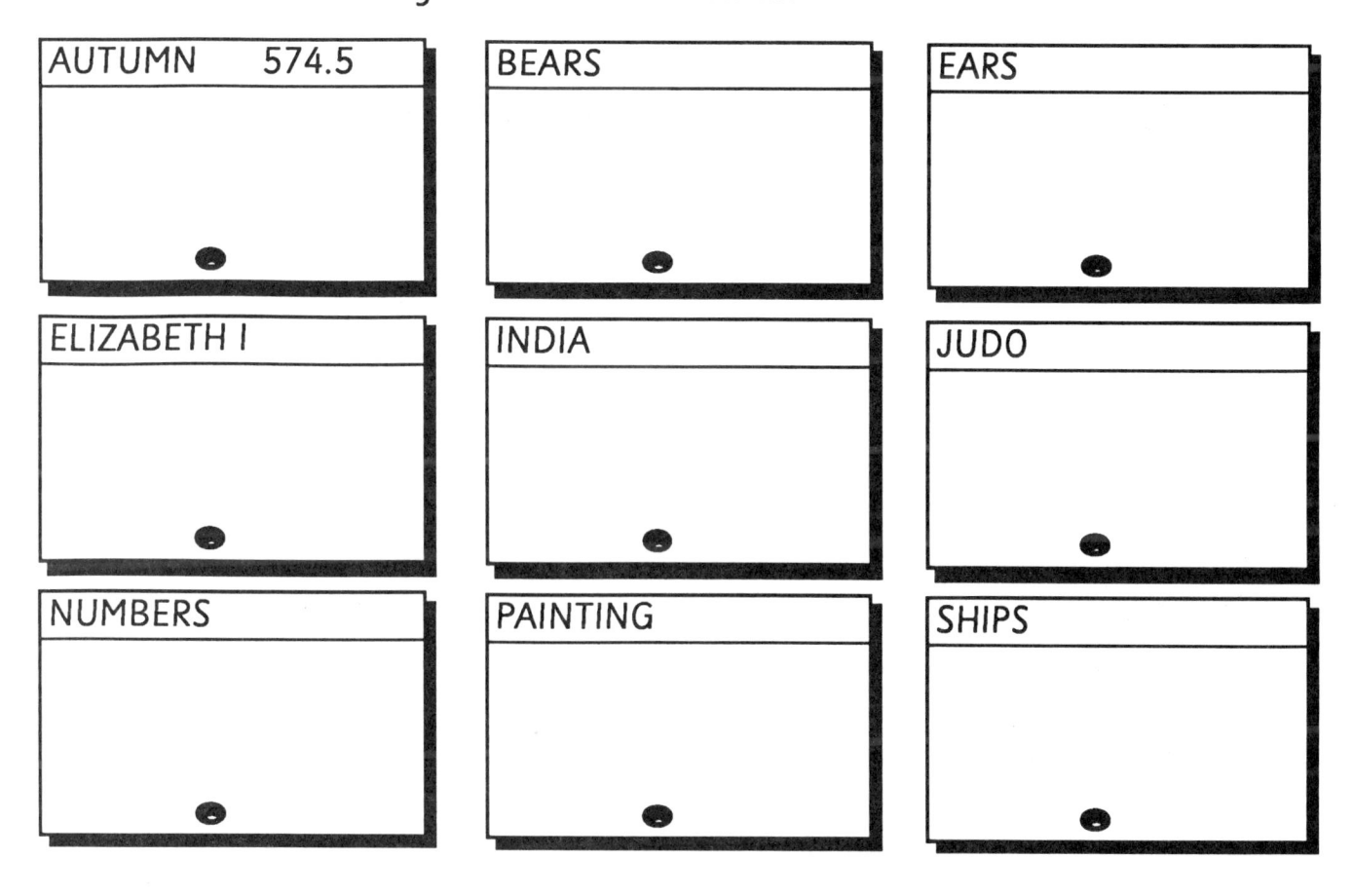

AUTUMN 574.5	BEARS	EARS
ELIZABETH I	INDIA	JUDO
NUMBERS	PAINTING	SHIPS

- Look in your school's classified index for some titles of books on the following subjects. On the back of this sheet, draw a classified index card for each one.

TENNIS   SHARKS   INVENTIONS   ANCIENT EGYPTIANS
MOUNTAINS   FORESTS   SOLAR SYSTEM   BUDDHISM

Using a contents page - Ideas Page

Purpose

- All contents pages that classify information under chapter headings require interpretation if they are to be of any real use. This activity provides an opportunity for such interpretation, and in the process it makes clear that the information required may be scattered throughout the book under different headings.
- The contents page in this activity not only classifies the information in each chapter, but also has sub-headings indicating the main topics in each chapter.

Ways In

- Discuss with the children the function and variety of contents pages in fiction, poetry and information books.

Fiction books	Poetry books	Information books

- Using the contents pages of real books, point out that some are very straightforward, some gather information under headings and therefore require interpretation, and some give additional information through sub-headings.
- In pairs or small groups, children could search for contents pages in project books, to see if they can find an example of each kind mentioned above.

Helpful contents pages	Why?	Unhelpful contents pages	Why?

Activity Sheet

- Explain that the purpose of the activity is to help them use a complicated contents page to track down information in a book.
- If possible, acquire the book this page comes from and show its contents page in context. (See page 2 for details.)
- If any of the children in the class know about the aircraft referred to on the page, invite contributions.
- The children could work in pairs or small groups. When they have finished the quiz, pool the answers.

Developments

- Ask the children to find a contents page which is more difficult to use. Working in pairs, each child could write a contents page quiz for their partner.
- Children could find an information book without a contents page and write one for it.
- Ask small groups of children to look critically at the contents pages of their project books, sorting them into those they find the most helpful and those they find the least. Can they say why?
- Make sure that the children make contents pages for their own project folders, using headings to classify the information.

Answers

Topic	Page
Legends	6, 7
Sea planes	22-25
Before powered flight	6-10
Early aviators	14, 15
Careers	24
Military aircraft	16-22
German aircraft	16-21
Flight without wings	8, 9, 20, 21
Flight in sport	8
War	16-22
First aircraft	6-13
Animal experiments	8, 9

Using a contents page

• Work in a group. Read this contents page from a book about aircraft.

Contents

DREAMS OF FLIGHT	6	WORLD WAR 1	16

DREAMS OF FLIGHT — 6
Daedelus, Icarus, Bird flight, Flapping wing flight, Flying machines.

BALLOONS — 8
Animal aviators, Parachutes, André Garnerisn, Balloon racing.

GLIDING — 10
Sir George Cayley, Triplane glider, Aerial steam carriage, Ornithopter.

THE WRIGHT BROTHERS — 12
The Flyer biplane. Wing-warping, First successful flight.

FIRST AVIATORS — 14
Louis Bleriot, First airshow, Golden Flyer, Flying the Channel.

WORLD WAR 1 — 16
Military aircraft, German Taube, Fokker E. III, Sopwith Camel.

AIR BATTLES — 18
The Red Baron, British S.E.5a, Fokker DrI Triplane, Dogfights.

AIRSHIPS — 20
The Graf Zeppelin, The Hindenburg.

FLYING BOATS — 22
Boeing 314 Clipper, Princess.

FIRST AIRLINERS — 24
Commercial aviation, Airports, Tin Goose, First stewardesses.

A CONTENTS PAGE QUIZ

• Where would you look to find out about:

legends about flying?   pages 6 and 7   German aircraft?   _____
sea planes?   _____   flight without wings?   _____
before powered flight? _____   flight in sport?   _____
famous early aviators? _____   war?   _____
careers in flying?   _____   the first aircraft?   _____
types of military aircraft? _____   animal experiments?   _____

© Folens — IDEAS BANK – Information and Library Skills — 15

Using an index - Ideas Page

pages 28-29

Purpose

- Many indexes in children's information books have entries which require an unrealistic degree of prior knowledge: the words are unfamiliar and their meanings unknown.
- Because this is such a common experience for children, a similar index is included on the activity sheet. It demands prior knowledge of the subject (boats) which will be beyond all but the specialist. It is presented here so that you can discuss strategies to cope with it, for example refer to the page numbers cited by the reference, or use a dictionary.

Ways In

- Make sure each child has access to information books with indexes, preferably project books with which the children are familiar.
- Ask them to suggest the purpose of an index. Then ask them to say what they find difficult about using indexes. Let them refer to their project books to help them answer the questions. List their responses. This should establish the need to learn strategies to cope with a difficult index.

What indexes are for	Why I find them difficult

Activity Sheet

- Read the index with the children. Pause on words whose meaning is not clear. Use a dictionary to clarify the meaning.
- Which words were the most difficult? Why? Where else could they look for this information? This should demonstrate to the children that the index of a book is not always a simple way of finding information.
- Refer to the page numbers in the first box and talk about why they have been chosen. Let everyone attempt the next box individually. They could then finish the exercise in pairs.
- Check the answers, discussing the differences between the children's responses.

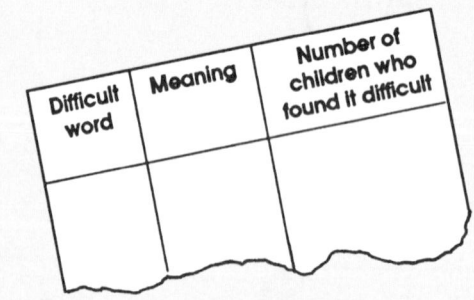

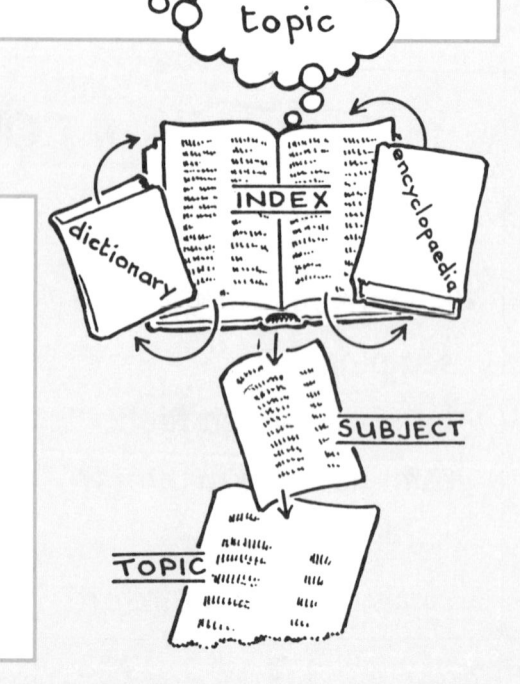

Difficult word	Meaning	Number of children who found it difficult

Developments

- Try to ensure that when children use an index for research they follow a focused approach: defining the heading under which the information is classified, then combing through the index to find suitable items, using a dictionary, or the book itself, for help with unfamiliar words.
- Some indexes are now grouped under sub-headings, and you may be able to find one to show the children.
- The children's own indexes for their project folders could be presented with sub-headings. Make a display of them.

16 © Folens

Using an index

- Read the index. In the boxes below, write the numbers of the pages you would use to research each subject.

Index

aircraft carriers	28	lifeboats	20-21
canoes	8, 10-11	Maoris	10
catamarans	19	narrow boats	28-29
clippers	18	Native Americans	10
coracles	8	oars	10, 16, 17, 21, 22, 23
dories	14		
dredgers	27	outriggers	11, 14
dugouts	8, 14	Oxford eight	16-17
Egyptians	8, 14	*Pachanga*	27, 24-25
ferry boats	26	Phoenicians	9
fishing boats	8, 10, 14, 15	propellers	12, 13, 25
galleys	17	punts	23
gondolas	22-23	rafts	8, 10, 11
Greeks	17	reed boats	8-9
houseboats	28, 29	rowing boats	16, 17
hydrofoils	24	sailing boats	18-19
icebreakers	27	sampans	17
Inuit	10	steamboats	12-13
jukungs	14-15	swamp cruisers	25
junks	26-27	trawlers	15
kayaks	10	Vikings	16

Sea transport
28, 26, 24-25, 18-19, 12-13, 16

Sport and recreation

Before boats with engines were invented

Living on boats

Careers in shipping

Motorboats

Boats that glide (no engine)

The fishing industry

Boats with special jobs

How information is organised on the page - Ideas Page

Purpose

- The purpose of this activity is to make children more aware of the way information is organised in the books they use in the classroom and library. They will look at not only the variety of techniques employed but also the purposes of each technique.
- The children will be encouraged to think harder about how design reflects – or, in some cases, works against – the needs of the reader.

Ways In

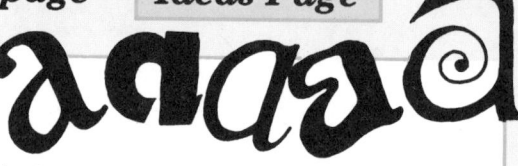

- Explain to the children that authors and designers of information books, magazines and leaflets use many ways of presenting information.
- Show the children two contrasting designs for a double-page spread, one very simple (a paragraph of text, a picture and caption) and one very complex (an Usborne book). Ask the children to say what the immediate difference is, and which needs the most skill and knowledge to read.
- Talk about the key role of the designer in deciding how the text and artwork is presented on the page.
- Explain to the children the following two principles:

Reading

SKIM → For a general impression.

SCAN → To find specific items.

A class graph

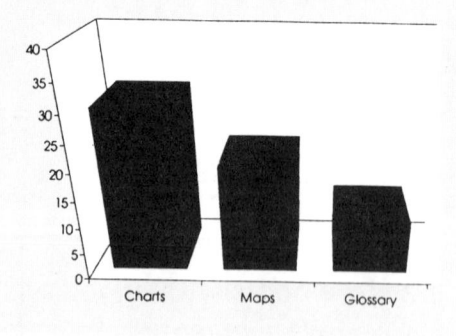

To show which techniques were used most in our books.

Activity Sheet

- Talk briefly about the items in the boxes, illustrating each with examples from books. Ask the children to find examples before starting the activity.
- Give the children a time limit of 20-30 minutes to complete the activity. They could work in pairs.
- Add up the class' score for each item, thereby revealing which design techniques are used the most. Graphs and other visual representations could be used to display this information.

Developments

- As part of their project or library study, give each pair of children two sheets of A3 paper. Ask them to make a rough design of a double-page spread of information on the first page, using at least five of the design techniques investigated earlier. Use the second sheet for a fair copy. The children could explain their decisions to the rest of the class. Designs could be displayed.
- Ask the children to bring in magazines from home, to examine their design features in the same way.
- Some children could look at information books for 5–7 year olds and evaluate the appropriateness of their design features for this age group.

Our survey. Design features in the newspaper

Number | Headings | Sub-headings | Introductory Paragraph | Photographs | Maps | More than 2 type faces

Newspaper

© Folens

Skim and scan

- How many examples of these can you find in your project books?
- Keep a tally in the boxes below each time you find one.

Main heading.	Information in boxes with different coloured background.	Labelled pictures or diagrams.
Introductory paragraph.	Extended captions to pictures or diagrams.	Tables, charts or graphs.
Sub-headings.	More than two typefaces.	Maps.
Headings or sub-headings in the form of a question.	Key words highlighted and explained in a glossary.	If you have discovered anything else, record it here.
Text broken into small parts.	A picture sequence or flow chart.	

© Folens IDEAS BANK – Information and Library Skills

Formulating key questions - Ideas Page

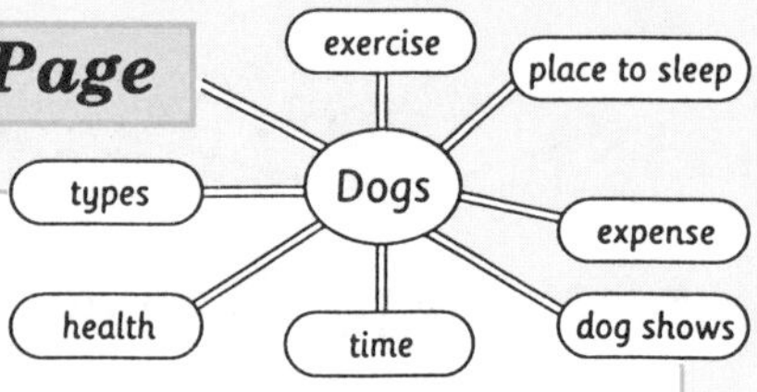

Satellite diagram: Dogs — exercise, place to sleep, types, expense, health, time, dog shows

Purpose

- A basic research skill is the ability to formulate key questions to frame an enquiry. This activity shows children a simple way of doing this.
- It uses a brainstorming technique which has wide applications, both as a planning and thinking tool and as an initial sorting device for ideas.
- The activity is directed towards personal research, away from a reliance on teachers' help.

Ways In

- Explain to the class that you are going to show them a basic technique to use when they start to research any subject.
- To introduce satellite drawings, draw one on the board or on a large sheet of paper, like the one on page 21. Choose a child to help you whom you know has a personal interest in and some knowledge of a particular subject.
- You could make another one to which the whole class could contribute, using the class project.
- Show the class how satellite subjects can be turned into key questions. Use 'Who? When? What? Where? Why? Which? How?' questions; call them 'Key questions for research'. The children could help you frame these questions.

Speech bubble: What food does my dog need to keep healthy?

Key questions for research	
Who?	Who do I go to when my dog is ill?
When?	When do I feed my dog?
What?	
Where?	
Why?	
Which?	
How?	

Activity Sheet

- Ask the children to think of a subject they would each like to explore. Ensure that they choose something that can be easily researched using the school's resources. They write this in the middle of their satellite drawing, and then think of three satellite subjects.
- The children should write their questions in the three speech bubbles.

Sidebar: How could my research be presented? — Question and answer sheet; Project folder; Recorded interviews

Developments

- As the children finish their satellite diagrams, they could take one or two books from the library to carry out their research.
- Let them answer in rough first. Then decide with the class how the research could be presented: work through examples from several children's projects. Presentation styles might include a simple question and answer sheet, a personal project folder or book, or a taped version of the research.
- Leave copies of this activity sheet in the school library and in the classroom to stimulate personal research.
- Use the basic shape of a satellite drawing for a display on the topics you intend to cover in the class project. Invite children to add speech bubbles containing their own questions.

© Folens

Key questions

If you wanted to know more about dogs, you could start by making a satellite drawing.

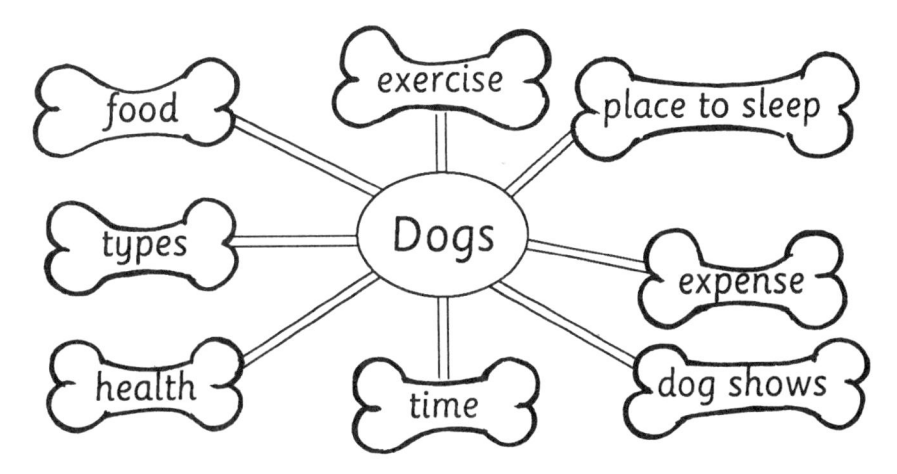

Satellite drawing with "Dogs" at the centre and bones labelled: food, exercise, place to sleep, types, expense, health, time, dog shows.

Each part of the subject can then be turned into a question:

food could become: **What food does my dog need to keep healthy?**

- Use this satellite drawing to start research on a subject.
- Choose three things about the subject and turn them into questions.

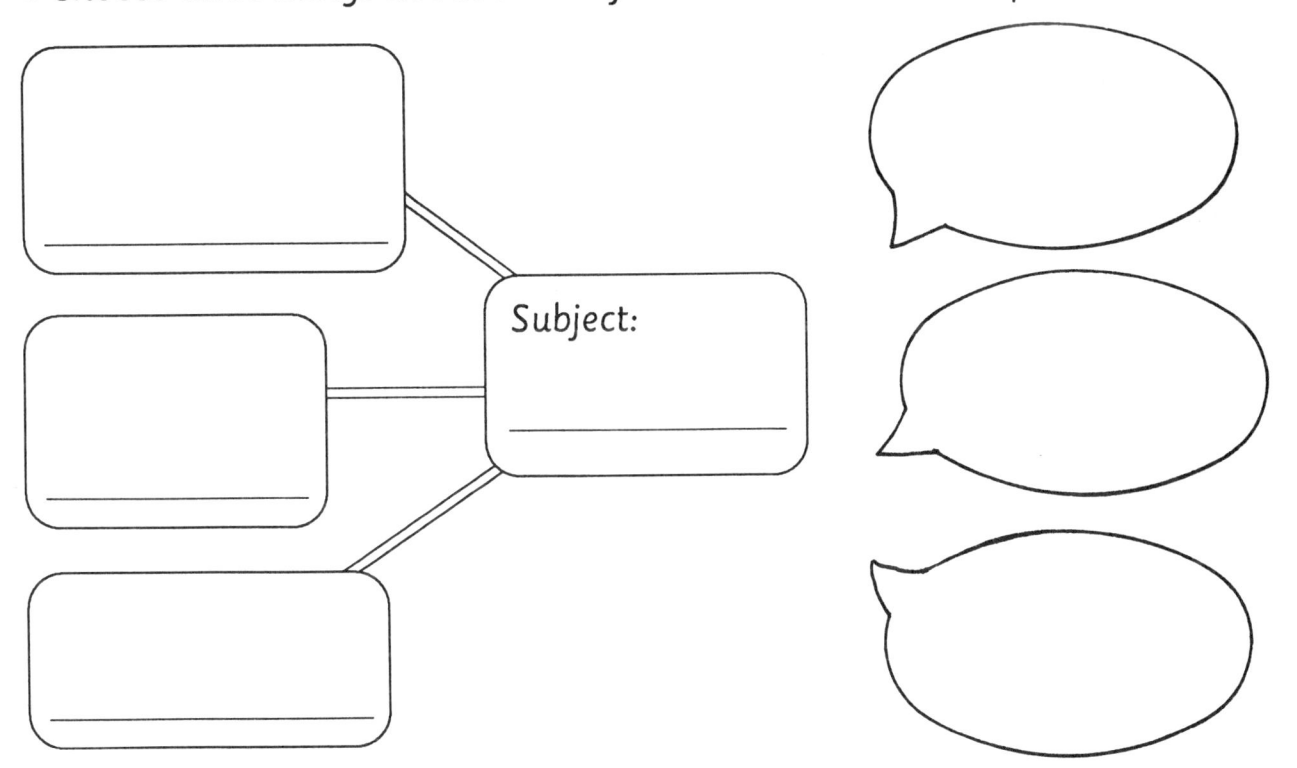

Subject: _____

© Folens   IDEAS BANK – *Information and Library Skills*   21

Types of text 1 - Ideas Page

Purpose

- This activity looks at the different forms of language most commonly used in information texts: explanations (non-chronological), narrative (chronological, eg stories, life cycles) and instructions (usually chronological, eg a recipe – but can be non-chronological, such as the example on the activity sheet).
- It aims to extend children's knowledge about how written language works. From this example, the children should learn that forms of writing imply some sort of distance between text and reader.

Explanation? Narrative? Instructions?

Ways In

- Explain that the purpose of this activity is to help the children to understand the way in which information books are written. Point out that it focuses on the most commonly used forms of language: explanation, narrative and instruction.
- Find an example of each style, preferably from books the children are using in their projects. Read these aloud, telling them clearly which passage is in which style.
- Pause at the end of the second passage and ask the children to identify the main differences in tone and structure between the passages, and to say which they find easiest to follow. Do the same after the third passage. Note the main differences on a chart.

Passage 1	Passage 2	Passage 3
Gives information.	Tells a story, has invented characters.	Is a list. Tells you what to do. Has no explanations.

Activity Sheet

- Briefly explain the subject of the activity sheet – air pollution – and find out what the children know about this subject.
- Ask the children to read the three passages and talk in pairs about the way the texts differ. They could write notes on the back of the sheet under the following headings:

Differences	
What they say	How they say it

- Allow the children to share their results. List and display the most common answers.
- Finally, ask the children to identify the three types of text by labelling each example.

Developments

- The children should now apply their knowledge of language forms to their project books, as well as other information books and library material. How many examples of each can the children find in these sources?
- In the process, the children will encounter other kinds of text type (lists, descriptions, sub-headings, text clarified with bullet points). These can be discussed and listed too.
- When children are planning to write up their research, remind them to consider the different forms of text available to them.

Explanation? Narrative? Instruction?

- Talk about how these three examples differ in the way they present the information. Label each example with a different word from the title above.

Acid Rain

Mrs Brown puts coal on the fire. Mr Brown starts his car. Both cause fumes to rise in the air. Later, rain falls. It mixes with the gases caused by the fumes and falls as acid rain. Slowly it eats into trees and plants, causing damage. Mr and Mrs Brown read about this in the newspaper. "What a terrible thing this acid rain is," they say.

Type of text: ☐

It gives the information like a story.

Action on Air Pollution

What can you do?
1. Leave the car at home. Walk.
2. Get a catalytic converter for your car.
3. Use smokeless fuel.
4. Use less electricity at home and at work.
5. Find out more about Greenpeace and Friends of the Earth.

Type of text: ☐

It tells you what to do.

Fossil Fuel

Much of today's air pollution is caused by the burning of oil and coal. These fossil fuels make gases which pollute the air. When rain falls it mixes with these gases, creating acid rain. Acid rain damages plant life, which in turn damages insect, fish, bird and animal life.

Type of text: ☐

It presents and explains facts.

© Folens   IDEAS BANK – *Information and Library Skills*

Types of text 2 - Ideas Page

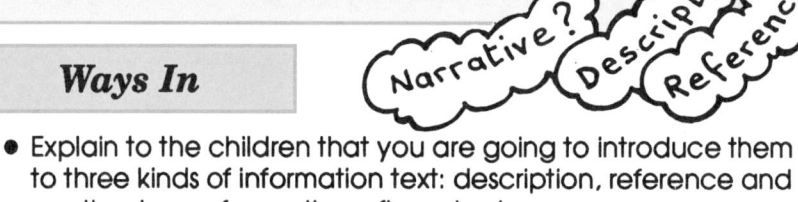

Narrative? Description? Reference?

Purpose

- This activity looks at three forms of language commonly found in information texts: narrative (chronological, eg flow charts), descriptions, and references (both non-chronological).
- The children should gain additional insights from these activities:
  - that poorer texts often mix text types indiscriminately in one passage
  - that each text type can have several different registers (tone, style, structure)
  - that some subjects often have their own distinct registers.
- The activity should enable the children to develop a more critical view of the texts they use.

Ways In

- Explain to the children that you are going to introduce them to three kinds of information text: description, reference and another type of narrative – flow charts.
- Read aloud or show them a clear example of each, preferably from the class' project books or an encyclopaedia.
- Pause after the second passage and discuss the differences in tone and structure between the pieces. Do the same after the third example. Note the main differences on a chart.

Differences		
Description	**Reference**	**Narrative**
Tells you what it looks like and …	Gives essential information.	Tells you what happened.

Activity Sheet

- Read the introduction on the sheet, then ask the children to discuss differences and to label the texts in the spaces provided. They could work in pairs.
- The second, descriptive passage on rain contains a number of words which might prove unfamiliar to some children. Do not explain the meanings of the words, but take this opportunity to link this with dictionary work.
- Provide an opportunity for the children to report back. Check that the children have labelled the passages appropriately.

Developments

- Recap on this activity and 'Explanation? Narrative? Instruction?' (pages 22–23). List the main types of text that the children will find in their information books:

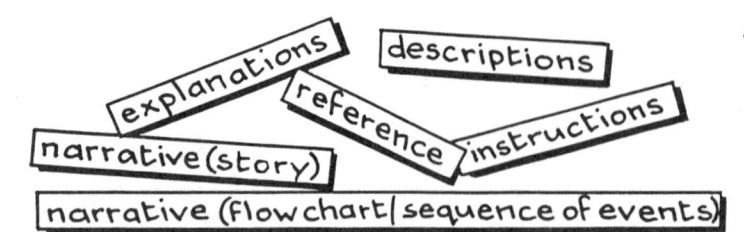

  - explanations
  - descriptions
  - reference
  - instructions
  - narrative (story)
  - narrative (flow chart / sequence of events)

- Display the list in the classroom. Leave space to add other examples of text types as the children discover them.
- When the children are writing up their project research, remind them of the text types available to them. Refer to the list you have displayed.

Narrative? Description? Reference?

- Talk about how these examples differ in the way they present information.
- Label the three examples using words from the title.

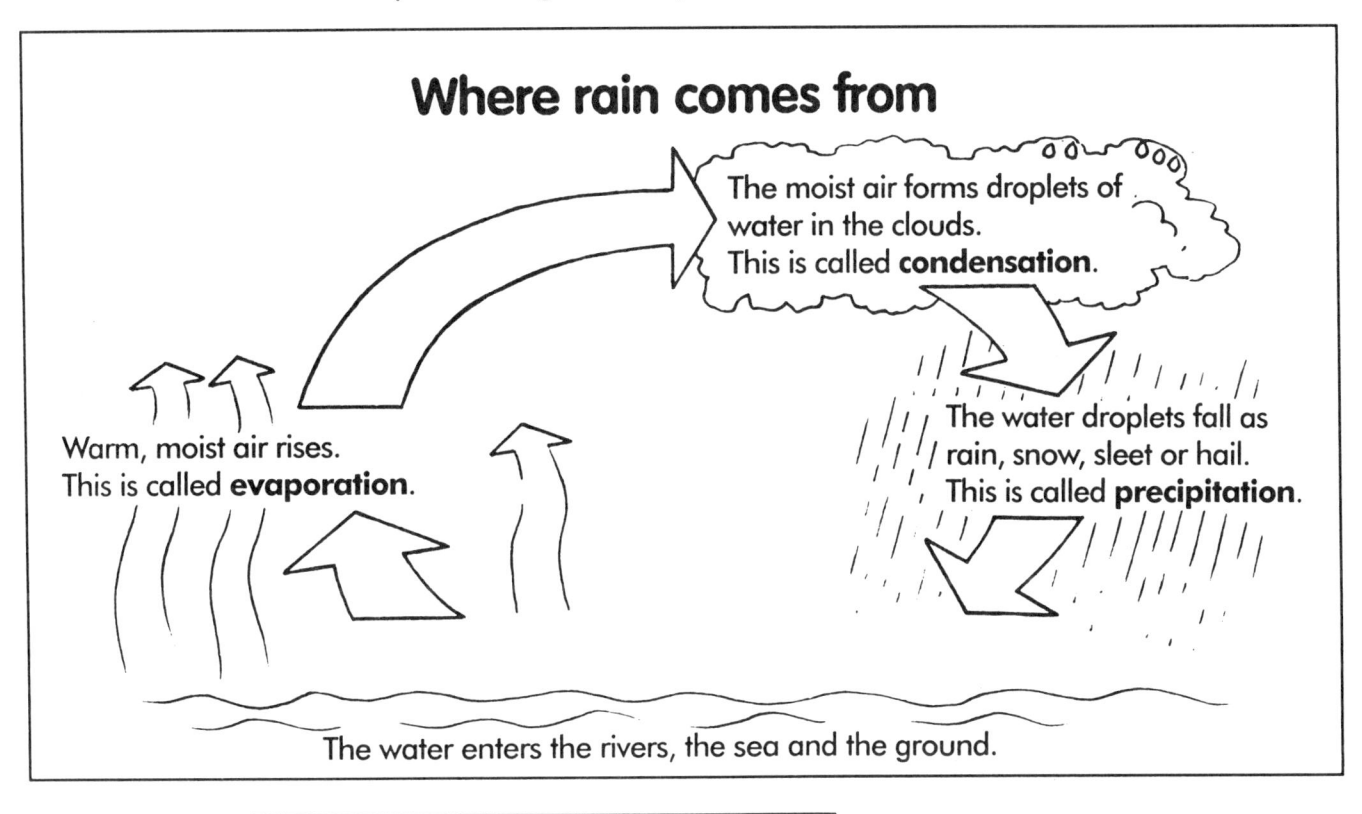

Where rain comes from

Warm, moist air rises. This is called **evaporation**.

The moist air forms droplets of water in the clouds. This is called **condensation**.

The water droplets fall as rain, snow, sleet or hail. This is called **precipitation**.

The water enters the rivers, the sea and the ground.

Type of text: ☐

It gives the information in a sequence of events.

From an encyclopaedia:

Rain – precipitation as separate drops of water. Droplets condense from water vapour in the air. They accumulate into drops which fall to the Earth's surface.

Type of text: ☐

It defines the terms or subject, giving its basic meaning.

What is rain?
Rain always falls as drops of water from clouds, but can take many forms. It can be only a shower, quick and light. It can be a heavy downpour. It can be just a fine drizzle. If it is very fine it feels like a mist. When rain is heavy and continuous, rivers may overflow, causing floods.

Type of text: ☐

It describes something.

Types of text 3 - Ideas Page

Purpose

- This activity extends the children's recognition of text types to include diary writing, autobiography and biography.
- It will help them to understand the basic grammatical difference between the texts: the use of first and third person pronouns characteristic of such writing.
- It will also help the children to make the link between primary sources (diaries and letters), with accounts of the same events in secondary sources, eg autobiographies and biographies.

Ways In

- Show some clear examples of these forms of writing. These are most likely to be in the history section, for example 'Famous People' series. The children may know of the most famous child's diary of all, Ann Frank's.
- Talk about children's experiences, diaries and personal letters, emphasising that they are written when events occur, and use the first person pronouns 'I', 'me', 'we' and 'us'. Write this information on a large chart.

Diary	Autobiography	Biography

- Talk about autobiographies, emphasising their retrospective and selective nature, and the use of the same pronouns as in diaries. Add this to your notes on the chart.
- Talk about biographies, reading one or two extracts aloud. Note on the chart that these are written by another person and therefore use the pronouns 'he', 'she', 'him', 'her', 'they' and 'them'.

Activity Sheet

- Ask the children to discuss how the autobiographical account differs from the diary account, and whether the biographer (in the last passage) made best use of the primary source material. The diary account is genuine. The other two texts are imagined and modern.
- Share the children's insights with the whole class.

Diary	Autobiography
A day-to day account.	A story of your life.
Usually a secret book.	A book to be read by others.
Written at the time.	Written later or after the events.

Developments

- Ask pairs of children to search for examples of these three kinds of writing, from history (information) books and biographical series.
- Ask the children each to write a diary entry for something that has happened to them in the past week. They could rewrite it as though it came from their autobiography. Children could then give these to a partner, to use them as 'primary sources' for a biographical piece.

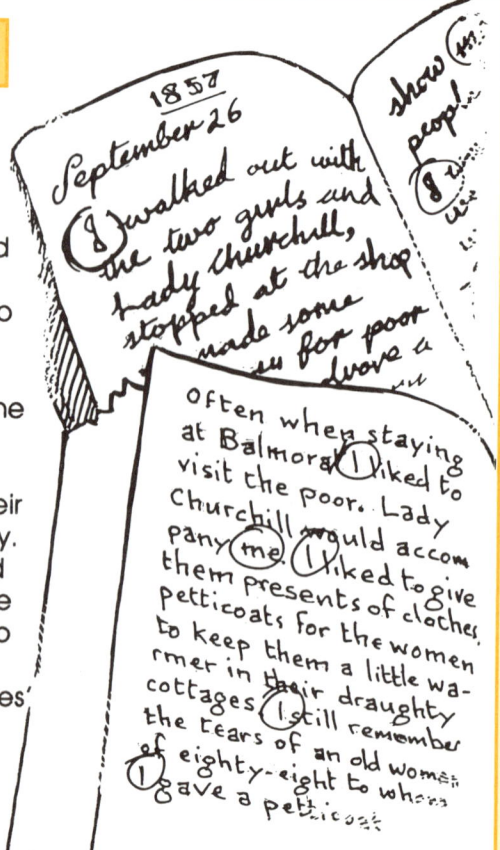

Queen Victoria visits the poor

- Talk about how these three accounts are different.

Diary: recording events as they happen.
On 26th September 1857, Queen Victoria wrote this in her diary:

... I walked out with the two girls and Lady Churchill, stopped at the shop and made some purchases for poor people and others; drove a little way, got out and walked up the hill to Balnacroft, Mrs. P. Farquharson's, and she walked around with us to some of the cottages to show me where the poor people lived, and to tell them who I was. Before we went into any we met an old woman, who, Mrs. Farquharson said, was very poor, eighty-eight years old ...
I gave her a warm petticoat, and the tears rolled down her old cheeks, and she shook my hands, and prayed God to bless me: it was very touching ...

Autobiography: a story of one's own life.

Often, when staying at Balmoral, I liked to visit the poor. Lady Churchill would accompany me. I liked to give them presents of clothes, petticoats for the women to keep them a little warmer in their draughty cottages. I still remember the tears of an old woman of eighty-eight to whom I gave a petticoat. She shook my hand, she blessed me, and I was very touched.

Biography: the story of someone else's life.

One of the queen's pastimes at Balmoral was to visit the poor on the estate, sometimes accompanied by some of her children. She was made very welcome, for the clothes she gave them as presents were much needed. In her journal for September 1857 she records an encounter with an 88-year-old woman who cried and blessed her: ' ... it was very touching,' she writes, revealing what these visits meant to her.

- Circle the words 'I', 'we', 'my' and 'me' in the first two extracts, and 'she' and 'her' in the last.
- What do they tell you about who wrote the passages, and when?

Making and using a glossary - Ideas Page

Purpose

- An increasing number of information books for children have glossaries, usually at the back of the book. Sometimes these appear as mini-glossaries on each page.
- These glossaries explain technical terms, key concepts and subject-specific vocabulary used in the text. Without them, a text's vocabulary may be too difficult.
- This activity, which uses a text full of technical terms, key concepts and specialist language, demonstrates how important a glossary can be in helping the reader to make sense of a text.
- It also requires the children to construct their own glossary using dictionaries and reference books. This will test the children's understanding of glossaries.

Ways In

- Explain to the children that glossaries list those words in a book which readers may not understand.
- Find examples of glossaries – preferably in books currently used in the classroom – and talk about them with the children. Explain that you will demonstrate how glossaries can improve their understanding of a page.

Book	Word	Definition	Comments
My First Weather Book.	Thermometer	Something you use to measure the temperature.	Simple for children.
Dictionary	Thermometer	Instrument in which a ...	Complicated for an adult.

Activity Sheet

- Explain that the text on the activity sheet gives information on how local weather measurements are made (without using satellites).
- Read the text aloud, pointing out that the bold words are technical terms which need explaining to a non-specialist. Each unknown word implies a question: 'What is ... ?' (eg 'What is a barometer?'). A glossary provides the answers.
- Show the class that the glossary lists words in alphabetical order.
- The children could work in pairs or small groups. They should attempt to provide definitions for the glossary, using dictionaries and reference books.
- Gather the class together and compare some definitions of each word, emphasising clarity, brevity and accuracy as key elements in any good glossary.

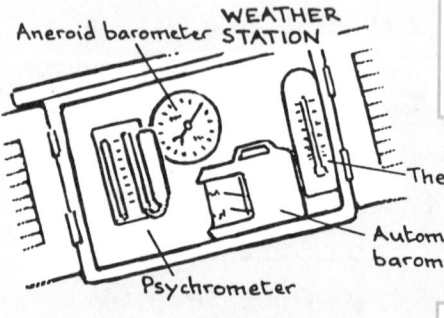

```
A = anemometer
B = barometer
F = forecast
H = humidity
```

Developments

- The children could write their own glossaries for a short book or a complex page, perhaps aimed at younger children.
- The children could be encouraged to underline or copy difficult words whenever they are reading a text. They could then write a short glossary for the passage.
- They could also look critically at existing glossaries in information books, and rewrite definitions that they feel are unclear or inaccurate.

Making and using a glossary

- Read the information and complete the glossary.

A Weather Station

A weather station is a place where scientists collect data about the weather using precise measuring instruments. The data is used to **forecast** the weather.

Weather has many different elements, each of which can be measured. For example, to measure **temperature**, you would use a **thermometer**. A **barometer** measures **atmospheric pressure**.

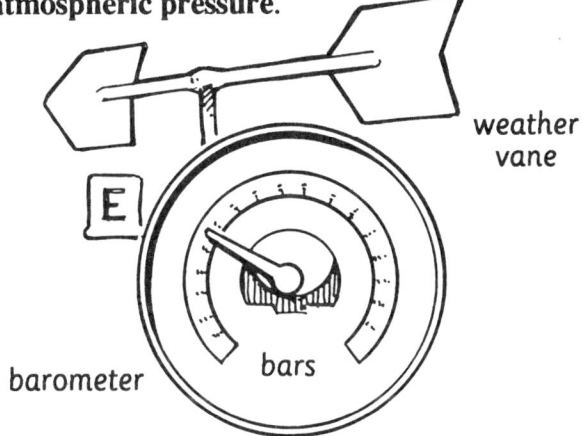

Forecasters also need to know the amount of **humidity** in the air: they find this information with a psychrometer. Wind direction is important, too, and a **wind vane** shows this. Wind speed is measured with an **anemometer**.

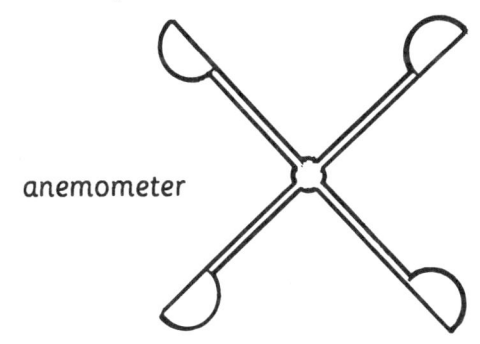

The weather station will also have a **rain gauge** to measure the amount of **rainfall**.

Glossary

anemometer
cups or an arrow on a pivot spin in the wind, giving a speed reading on a dial in knots.

atmospheric pressure
the weight of the atmosphere as measured by a barometer.

barometer _____

forecast _____

humidity _____

rainfall _____

rain gauge _____

temperature _____

thermometer _____

wind vane _____

Finding the main idea 1 - Ideas Page

Purpose

- This activity aims to help children focus on key words and ideas in a text.
- This skill will enable them to make notes from research texts.
- It helps the children to organise their note-taking into thematic groups.
- It demonstrates that notes do not have to be scribbled and can take many forms, for example a chart or table.

Ways In

- If the children have not had experience of underlining, you may wish to introduce it by underlining three different aspects of text – as required here.
- Discuss with the children how they make notes. Emphasise that note-taking has two functions: to isolate key ideas and to act as an *aide-mémoire*.

What I want to remember	Why
A castle has thick walls.	It shows how strong the castle was.
A castle has small windows.	Proves they had to defend the castle.

Questions the class want to ask.

- Where did the people live?
- Why were the walls thick?
- Whose castle is it?
- What happens there now?

Where can we find the answers?

Activity Sheet

- If possible, make an A3 enlargement of the activity sheet.
- Read the text through with the class.
- On the enlarged copy, demonstrate the underlining technique by underlining one example of each theme. Stress that you are underlining only those words that are important.
- The children should work in pairs. This ensures that they negotiate each underlining and therefore read the text more closely.
- Some children have a tendency to underline too much. They do not sort the main idea from the supporting details. If this happens, limit these children to, say, ten underlinings.
- As a class, compare which words the children have underlined, in which colours, and what they have entered into the columns below.

Architecture	How people lived	Defence
Keep	Banquets for the rich	Thick walls
Thick walls	Heating by log fires	Window slits
	Soldiers living in same building	Garrison chamber
	Sleeping in alcoves	Soldiers in castle
		Weapons and armour

Developments

- Ensure the children are using this skill on their project as soon as possible.
- Ask pairs of children to write five questions about the activity sheet passage to ask their partner, who has to try and answer from memory.

© Folens

Finding the main idea

- Read this passage about a castle.
    - Underline in red words to do with architecture.
    - Underline in blue words to do with how people lived.
    - Underline in green words to do with defence.

The Norman keep at Castle Hedingham, Essex, is often visited by children from local schools. This is partly because the building is in such good condition.

The walls are about ten feet thick. The windows are small, sometimes no more than slits. Both these features made it hard for enemy soldiers to break through the castle's defences.

The main feature inside is a magnificent arch supporting the ceiling of the great banqueting hall. The Earls of Oxford lived in the castle for 550 years. They entertained guests and had their meals in this hall. A huge log fire helped to keep them warm in winter.

Underneath the banqueting hall is the garrison chamber. The soldiers lived here. They made and stored their weapons and armour here. Also, food was cooked on this level.

Above the banqueting hall is another large room with alcoves. This is where the Earls, their families and servants slept.

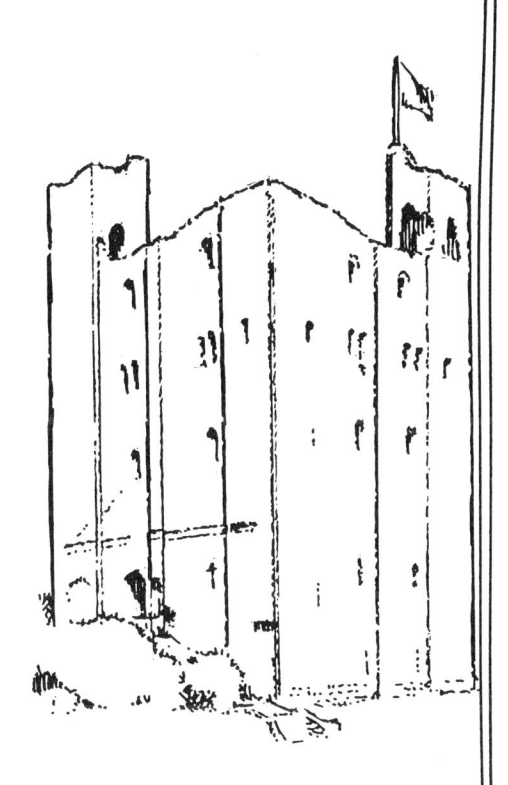

- Use the words or sections you have underlined to make notes in the boxes below.

Architecture	How people lived	Defence

Continue over the page ...

Finding the main idea 2 - Ideas Page

Purpose

- This activity shows the children how to make notes by summarising the main idea of a paragraph in note form.
- It builds on previous note-taking work (underlining), but shows a more conventional and flexible approach.
- It demonstrates that note-taking is the bridge between reading for information and writing up research in one's own words.

Ways In

- Write the word FIRE on the board. Brainstorm to identify all the aspects of fire which might be found in an information book.
- If possible, compare the brainstorm with the ideas about fire in a general book – perhaps an encyclopaedia – to see to what extent the two coincide.

Subject	Words we thought of
Fire 	Heat, flames, burn, sticks, orange, red, damage, wick, engines, elements, fuel, light, warm, destroys

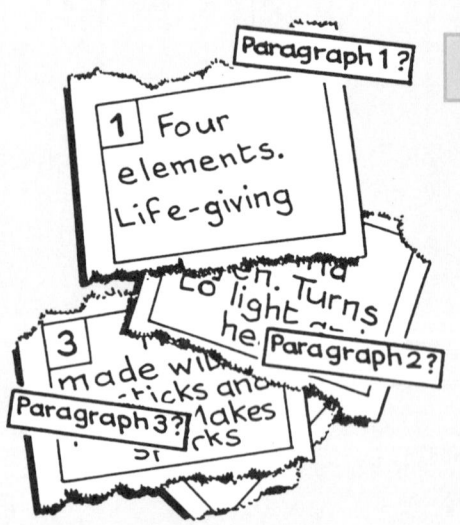

Activity Sheet

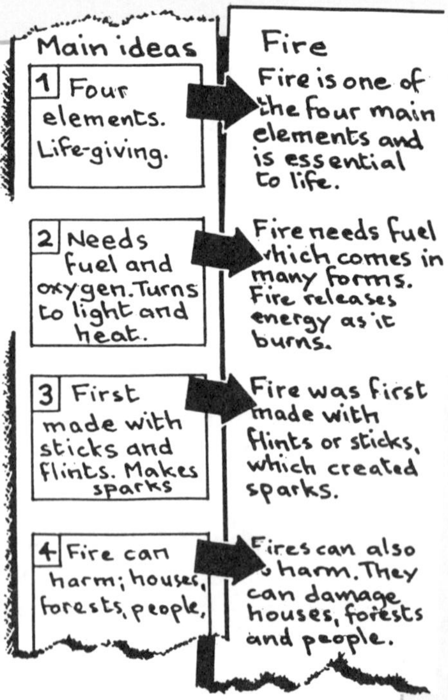

- Ask the children to work in pairs, to encourage discussion about the main idea of each paragraph and how best to express it in notes.
- Read the passage about fire aloud. Write an example sentence in the first box, such as 'One of the four elements. Life-giving'.
- Ask the children to attempt the second paragraph, writing their notes in rough first. Compare some of the notes with the class; agree on a best sentence and write it on the board for them to copy.
- The children could now work on the next three boxes.
- As they finish, check their answers. If necessary, ask them to look again at the passage and redraft their notes.
- Collect the class' completed sheets. Allow a day or two for the information in the text to become assimilated. Then give out the completed sheets and ask the children to fold them down the dotted line. Using their notes and without referring to the original text, they should then write a summary of the text in their own words.
- Show how the text could be set out in paragraphs and linked to make a complete passage. Once the children have done this, they could compare their texts with the original passage.

Developments

- Use this approach in class projects. Use key passages and ask the children to number the paragraphs. Remind them how to write a main idea as short notes.
- They could then write a summary based on their notes.

Main ideas	Fire
1 Four elements. Life-giving.	Fire is one of the four main elements and is essential to life.
2 Needs fuel and oxygen. Turns to light and heat.	Fire needs fuel which comes in many forms. Fire releases energy as it burns.
3 First made with sticks and flints. Makes sparks	Fire was first made with flints or sticks, which created sparks.
4 Fire can harm; houses, forests, people.	Fires can also harm. They can damage houses, forests and people.

32

© Folens

Ideas in boxes

- Write the main idea of each paragraph in the boxes.
- Fold the page down the dotted line.
- Use the notes in the boxes to write a passage about fire.

FIRE

Fire is one of the four main elements of life. The others are earth, air and water. Without fire there would be no heat or light, and the planet Earth would be a dead, cold, dark place.

Fire needs two things in order to burn: fuel and oxygen. The fuel comes in many forms, for example, as a liquid (eg cooking oil, petrol), as a solid (eg wood, coal) and as a gas (eg propane gas). The energy stored in the fuel is turned into heat and light as it burns.

It is thought that our distant ancestors discovered fire when they made sparks between two flints, or by rubbing sticks together. Imagine their surprise – fear, even – when they saw fire for the first time.

Fire keeps us warm, but it can also be an enemy. Think of volcanoes, forest fires, houses being burned down, people dying from severe burns. It kills and destroys.

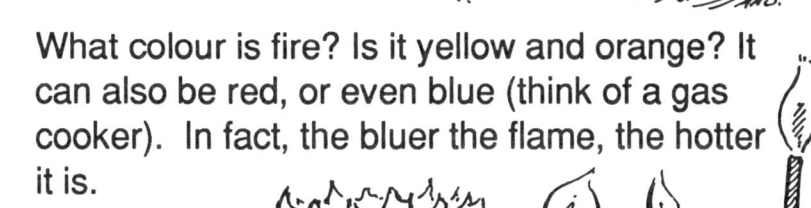

What colour is fire? Is it yellow and orange? It can also be red, or even blue (think of a gas cooker). In fact, the bluer the flame, the hotter it is.

Main ideas

1.

2.

3.

4.

5.

© Folens — IDEAS BANK – Information and Library Skills — 33

Comparing texts on the same subject - Ideas Page

Encyclopaedia Reference Book

Purpose

- Children need to learn that it is unwise to rely on the work of one author alone. Authors are selective and emphasise different aspects of any one subject.
- This activity reinforces their work with a selection of information texts, and guides them in note-taking from more than one text.
- It should lead children to make a series of critical judgements:
  - Who is this text for?
  - Which text tells me most?
  - What has been missed out?
  - Which is the clearest?
  - Which is the best text for my purpose?

Ways In

- Show the children a selection of texts on one subject, preferably about Van Gogh, identifying their different authors and pointing out that each text will be different.
- Show the class prints of his pictures. Ask the children to talk about their characteristics, whether they like them and why.
- Ask the children where they would look if they wanted to find out about the artist's life. Explain that when students research, they often look at more than one source on the same subject. These often contain different information.

Activity Sheet

- Read both passages aloud.
- Look up any unfamiliar vocabulary.
- Ask the children to suggest example entries for each of the three columns at the bottom of the activity sheet, to lead them into the exercise.
- Children should work in pairs. When they have finished, pool the results. Make a large display of them.

Developments

- Encourage the children to use this form of note-taking when they carry out any research using more than one text. They can, of course, use more than three columns if they wish.
- If the activity sheet is used as part of an art project, the children could research Van Gogh's life from several sources and write their own encyclopaedia entry about him. Encourage the children to use visual resources, both for their research and for their encyclopaedia entry.

Vincent's Sunflowers Painting. He did this in 1888. It is now in the National Gallery, London.

34 © Folens

Comparing passages

- Talk about the differences between these two passages.

From an encyclopaedia

GOGH, Vincent van, 1853–1890. Dutch painter. Born in Zundert, Netherlands.

Worked for a time as a schoolmaster in England, before he took up painting ...

In 1886 he went to Paris. Became a friend of Gauguin. They worked together for a short time in Arles, Provence. One of the leaders of the Post-Impressionists, he painted still lifes and landscapes, for example *A Cornfield with Cypresses*, *The Yellow Chair* and self-portraits.

He cut off part of his earlobe, following a quarrel with Gauguin. He spent the last years of his life in asylums and committed suicide.

From an art reference book

Vincent van Gogh (1853–1890), the most famous of the Post-Impressionists, was an educated man. He even became a schoolmaster – and he is one of the great letter-writers of the nineteenth century.

He trained himself to paint by studying the work of other artists. The great paintings by which he is best known, for example *Sunflowers*, were all done in the last 29 months of his life, when he was often ill as a patient at a hospital in Arles.

These pictures are remarkable for their vivid sense of colour and their bold, flowing forms. Although he was poor while he lived, selling only one painting in his lifetime, Van Gogh's pictures today sell for many millions of pounds.

- Make notes in each column.

What both texts tell us.	What only the first tells us.	What only the second tells us.

Continue over the page ...

© Folens   IDEAS BANK – *Information and Library Skills*

Facts and opinions - Ideas Page

Purpose

- One of the most important skills in reading for information is to be able to separate fact from opinion.
- This activity aims to demonstrate to children that opinions can be checked against factual information if their reliability and validity is in doubt.
- It should help children to recognise that statements of opinion, especially spoken ones, often masquerade as fact.

Ways In

- Before the lesson, find a few short written passages – some factual, some opinionated – from various sources, including books and tabloid newspapers.
- Begin by reminding the children of the basic difference between statements of fact and opinion.
- Give the children some of the short passages and ask them to say which is fact and which opinion, and why.
- Display their suggestions on a chart.

Fact	Opinion

- Read out some more of the brief examples that you collected earlier. Discuss the differences between the two.

Developments

- Pairs of children could compile a Fact File related to their project.
- If appropriate, they could also write opinions (in speech bubbles) related to the Fact File for another pair of children to evaluate.
- Make a display of opinion speech bubbles on a pinboard, related to the class project. Underneath it, display project information books. Invite the children to check the factual basis of some of the opinions.
- Ask the children to bring in examples of opinionated writing from newspapers. They could underline those passages which they feel need to be checked for validity and reliability.

Activity Sheet

- Explain that the items listed in the Fact File come from a report in *The Times* newspaper (27th January 1994) which summarised facts gathered from a survey of social trends in Britain during the 1980s and early 1990s (*Social Trends: 1994 Edition*, HMSO). This represents information rooted in research: it is factual.
- The opinions expressed in the speech bubbles can all be checked against the facts in the Fact File.

ANSWERS:
1. Opinion   4. Fact
2. Fact   5. Opinion
3. Fact   6. Fact

- Children could work in pairs. Once they have completed the activity, team each pair with another to compare their results.
- Complete the activity with a whole class discussion, drawing out themes from any disagreements between the groups.

OPINION: I think people smoke more now.

FACT: I know people are spending less on tobacco. Fewer people are smoking.

Facts and opinions

- Are the statements below facts or opinions?
- Check them against the Fact File and tick the boxes.

1. People smoke as much now as they did in 1971.

Fact ☐ Opinion ✓

2. People save more these days.

Fact ☐ Opinion ☐

3. Britain is one of the least law-abiding countries in Europe.

Fact ☐ Opinion ☐

4. There is no evidence that standards in education are rising.

Fact ☐ Opinion ☐

5. Men are just as likely to be unemployed as women.

Fact ☐ Opinion ☐

6. There are now more children under the age of five at school.

Fact ☐ Opinion ☐

FACT FILE

■ Under-fives at school trebled from 1965 to 1992.	■ A third of women were unemployed in 1993, more than twice the proportion of men.
■ Spending on tobacco fell by a third between 1971 and 1992.	■ The proportion of school leavers without exam passes halved between 1975 and 1992.
■ In 1992, 4.8% of people's pay was saved. This is the highest percentage since records began.	■ Apart from Luxembourg, Britain has the highest number of prisoners in jail, per head of population.

© Folens IDEAS BANK – *Information and Library Skills* 37

The language of persuasion - Ideas Page

Purpose

- It is important that children begin to understand that:
  - information can be used to persuade readers to change their views, to approve of something, or to buy something
  - information may have other purposes than simply to inform
  - information can be partial and subjective, in order to achieve a particular end
  - the language used in some information texts, such as advertisements, is chosen to make the reader feel well-disposed towards the product or idea.

Ways In

- Before the lesson, collect some texts which set out to persuade, taken from newspapers, magazines, catalogues and brochures.
- Explain to the children that some kinds of information set out more to persuade the reader (to do or think something) than to inform in an objective way, and that therefore the purpose behind such texts is different.

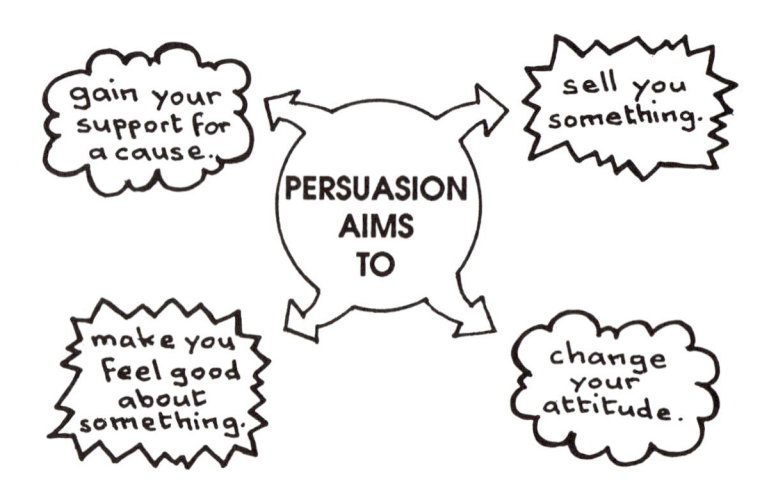

PERSUASION AIMS TO
- gain your support for a cause.
- sell you something.
- make you feel good about something.
- change your attitude.

- Read aloud the examples you have collected, asking the children to speculate on the purpose behind the 'information'.

For over 22 years Monarch has delivered holidays for the discerning traveller. Monarch continues to offer the highest standards of comfort at the finest resorts in the world. For 1994 Monarch bring you an even greater choice with Monarch Worldwide holidays in exotic locations.

Activity Sheet

- Read the hotel description to the children. Ask them to circle the persuasive vocabulary used in the first two lines, for example 'warm', 'golden', 'luxurious'.
- Explain that although this appears to be a full description of the hotel designed to inform holiday-makers of what they can expect, it leaves out many things that they would need to know, such as whether it is air-conditioned, or has a swimming-pool and other leisure activities.
- The children will then be ready to complete the chart on the activity sheet. They could work in pairs.
- End the activity by pooling the class' answers. Write them on a display chart.

Developments

- The children could look for advertisements in the media and carry out the same analysis.
- They could write their own persuasive descriptions, perhaps of their house or neighbourhood or school, which other children could then analyse in the same way.
- The children could pretend that they are staying at the hotel featured on the sheet. They could write a letter to a friend giving a wholly different picture of the hotel from that which is described.

The language of persuasion

• Talk about this advertisement for a holiday hotel.

The Holiday Hotel

The warm, golden sands of the lagoon are only a few steps away from this luxurious and friendly family hotel.

It has been run by the Patroli family for two generations and offers comfort, warmth and a uniquely friendly atmosphere.

The bedrooms are furnished in the traditional style, many with balconies overlooking the sea.

The restaurant is famous for its delicious variety of fish dishes.

At night you can eat by romantic candlelight, serenaded by Mr Patroli himself, who is celebrated for his folk-singing.

Relax on the golden sands by day and visit the picturesque village by night: it will be the holiday of your dreams.

Our opinion: a friendly, informal hotel beside a clean and spacious beach with easy access to local village sites.

• Copy and complete the chart.

Words to make you feel good:	Facts about the resort:	Things you are not told:
warm, golden, lagoon	It is by the beach.	How large it is.

Information to persuade - Ideas Page

Purpose

- Much of the information that children will encounter, particularly in the media, will be subjective, or even biased.
- This activity aims to guide children into considering:
  - the language of argument
  - the way that information can be used selectively
  - the intentions of the writer
  - how to recognise persuasive texts
  - how to construct such texts themselves.

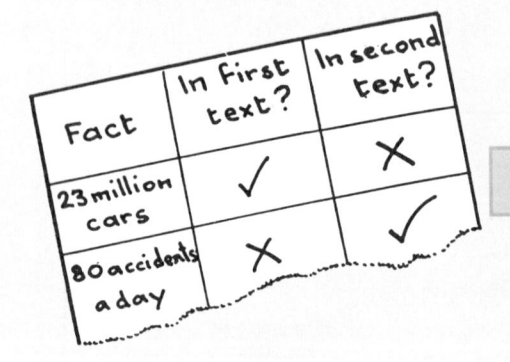

Ways In

- Introduce the subject dealt with on the activity sheet by asking the question: 'Are cars a good thing or are they more trouble than they are worth?' List the main points that emerge from the discussion in two columns.

For cars	Against cars
Convenient, faster journeys, private, something to be proud of.	Pollution, accidents, expensive.

- Pose the question: 'If you wanted to write an information book about cars, should you take a view for or against them?' This aims to provoke a discussion which raises the notions of bias and intention.

Activity Sheet

- Read both texts aloud. Explain the activity beneath them. The children can work in pairs on the same passage.
- What should emerge is that within both pieces a few facts are used to support two very different viewpoints. Summarise these facts on the board.
- Compare the children's responses to 'What the writer wants you to think'. The similarity of their answers should demonstrate intention, selective use of facts and bias.

Developments

- Hold a debate about cars, either in groups of four to six, or as a whole class, with speakers presenting partisan views.
- Encourage the children to write a summary of their thoughts on the subject. They should write it with the intention of persuading the reader to adopt their point of view. Such work could be developed into an advertising campaign. 
- Ask groups or pairs to think of ideas in response to the question at the end of the second piece on pollution: 'Is there a better alternative to the car?'
- If appropriate to your project, encourage the children to look through some of their library books for examples of information written to persuade, or information that they consider biased.

Information to persuade

- Read these two passages.

Cars: a convenience

There are something like 23 million cars in Britain today. Most households have one car; many have two. So why is the car so popular?

It is a cheap, comfortable and flexible way to travel anywhere you want. You can fit the journey around your needs, from a brief school run or shopping trip, to a fortnight's holiday tour. You are not dependent on timetables, the availability of seats or the location of stations. You just turn on the ignition and go.

Think of the freedom it gives you.

Cars: a pollutant

Before the last war, the manufacturers of cars could never have dreamed of the threat the vehicle now poses to modern life. Its undoubted convenience is paid for with a terrible price in death, maiming, disease and pollution of the environment.

In Britain today there are, on average, 80 serious road accidents a day.

Roads are becoming overcrowded and increasingly dangerous. Bigger roads have to be built at a huge cost to the taxpayer.

All this road-building causes great damage to the countryside. Animals and plant species are threatened.

Add to this the proven damage that car exhaust and petrol fumes do to human health, and you are left with the questions: Why do we do it? Isn't there a better alternative?

NOW • Complete these charts.

Cars: a convenience	
Facts	What the writer wants you to think

Cars: a pollutant	
Facts	What the writer wants you to think

Continue over the page ...

Using the question and answer form - Ideas Page

Purpose

- The question and answer form for presenting information is increasingly common, particularly in advertising and in booklets, leaflets and brochures published by various institutions. Many children's information books now use it.
- It is preferred because it reduces the social distance between reader and text: it appears more personal and accessible than a simple block of text.
- It is therefore valuable to present this form to the children for discussion. The children themselves have the option to use this form to present their own research.

Ways In

- Find some examples of the question and answer form in books, leaflets and advertising and use these to introduce the technique to the children.
- Prior to the introductory session, give a pair of children (who enjoy reading aloud) a suitable question and answer text. Ask them to rehearse it, one asking the questions, the other giving the answers. They can perform their piece after your introduction.

What do I want to find out about?	Which words give me clues?
The seashore	beach, sand, rocks, wild, stretch
What is the seashore like?	flat, edged with plants, tall cliffs

Activity Sheet

- Read the text about the seashore to the children.
- Explain how it has been rewritten as the question and answer passage. Read out the question and ask the children to read the answer aloud in reply.
- Ask them, in pairs, to rewrite the last paragraph as a question and answer text.

Developments

- Ask children to work in pairs. Each child should select a text related to their project and write a series of questions about it. The children then exchange their text and questions with their partners, and write the answers.
- If the questions and answers are written on separate pieces of paper or card, they can be used by other children. Mix up the questions and answers for each passage. Give the cards to a different pair, along with the original text, to match the questions to the answers.
- The children could bring in examples of question-and-answer texts. Make a display of the examples and the class' work.

Questions about the seashore.

Why does the seashore change?

Why are some shores dangerous?

Because the sea is always pounding the shore.

© Folens

Questions and answers

The seashore

The seashore can take many different forms. It can be a sandy beach where you can sunbathe and play. It can be rocky and wild. It can be one long stretch of coast or it can be a series of large bays and small coves.

Some shores will be flat, edged with plants; others will have tall cliffs where seabirds nest.

Seashores change. The sea is always pounding on the shore. Over time, the sea turns stones into sand; it makes rock crumble and it creates caves. It can cause cliffs to fall and whole coastlines can be eroded. Sometimes the sea adds land to the shore.

Some shores are dangerous: the sea can hide sharp rocks. Lighthouses warn ships to keep a safe distance.

This passage could have been written in a question and answer form.

Q What does the seashore look like?

A It can be sandy or rocky. It can stretch for miles or be a series of bays and coves. It can be flat or have tall cliffs.

- Answer the question:

Q Do seashores always stay the same?

A _____

- Turn over. Write questions and answers for the last paragraph of the passage.

- Turn another passage into the question and answer form.
- Find a book which uses this form.

Ways of presenting information - Ideas Page

Purpose

- Children learn to read information in many forms. This activity sheet refers to several of these. By talking about and using these forms in their own work, children will better understand how each form works.
- This activity can be a planning tool for the children to refer to when they consider how to present information in project and other work.

Ways In

- Explain to the children that you are going to talk about the many different means (verbal, audio, visual) by which authors and designers of information texts present information. Tell them that many of these styles can be used by the children in their own work.
- Demonstrate the importance of variety to presentation. Show an information book which has only print and very few design features. Contrast it with another book or a magazine spread which uses many different forms and is imaginative in its design. Ask the children to say what the differences are, which they prefer and why.

Book	Magazine	Preference

How does our class present information?

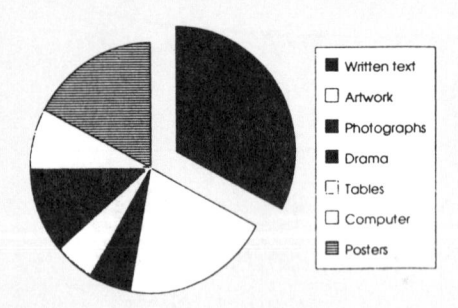

(pie chart: Written text, Artwork, Photographs, Drama, Tables, Computer, Posters)

Activity Sheet

- Talk briefly about each item on the sheet. Explain the activity to the children.
- The children should work in pairs, explaining to each other when and how they used the forms which they have ticked.
- At the end of the activity, share some of the responses with the class.

Developments

- Which were the most common ways of presenting information? Was this surprising? Record the information graphically.
- If the children are planning their own projects, they could use this sheet to help them in their discussions.
- Make a poster or a display of the activity sheet to remind the class of the choices available to them.
- Let groups of children check their current project books and library resources against the sheet, to see which forms of presentation appear most frequently.
- Groups could write each style on a separate slip of paper. They could then arrange them in order of preference, through discussion. Present the results to show how the class prefers to receive information.

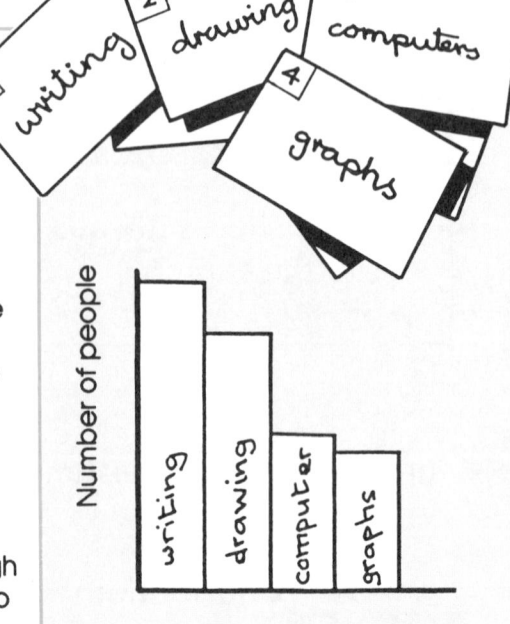

(bar chart: Number of people vs Order of preferences — writing, drawing, computer, graphs)

Ways of presenting information

- Tick the boxes if you have used any of these in your own work.

written text ✓	diagrams ☐	artwork ☐
photographs ☐	pie or bar charts ☐	graphs ☐
tables ☐	3-D models ☐	time-line ☐
audio-tape ☐	video-tape ☐	a scripted talk (with slides or OHPs if you wish) ☐
leaflet or brochure ☐	computer ☐	something else? Write them over the page. ☐

NOW
- Explain to a partner how you used these.
- Talk with your partner about any styles you could have used instead.

What I thought about my project - Ideas Page

Purpose

- Children work through many different projects and topics during their primary school education. They should be given opportunities to reflect on their individual performance within the projects, and to express their thoughts and feelings about them.
- The activity covers the following aspects of self-assessment:
  - indicating what most needs to be remembered
  - identifying areas of confusion
  - being aware of areas of the project not yet covered
  - identifying key books from library research
  - speculating on the reasons for choosing the project.
- In the process of making this assessment, the children will be expressing a preference and reviewing the ground covered in the project. This will give them an overview of what can often seem to have been a fragmented experience.

Ways In

- The sheet is designed to be used at the end of a project.
- The children should have all their project work to hand, and the reference books that they used during the project.
- Briefly remind the children of what you planned for the topic or project, what you set them to find out through library work and what ground has been covered during the project.

Activity Sheet

- Invite the children to present examples in response to some of the box headings.
- Encourage the children to talk in groups of two or three about their responses to each question before they write in the boxes. This will help them to consider their responses.
- When the children have finished, share some of the responses with the rest of the class. List some.
- When tackling 'But what still puzzles me is ...', consider whether you need to respond to these individually or whether a class discussion would be better. You could allow children to work in pairs to help each other with this section.
- The last item on the sheet, 'I talked about this sheet with ...', is a simple device to make sure that the personal responses recorded on the sheet are shared in a one-to-one conversation.

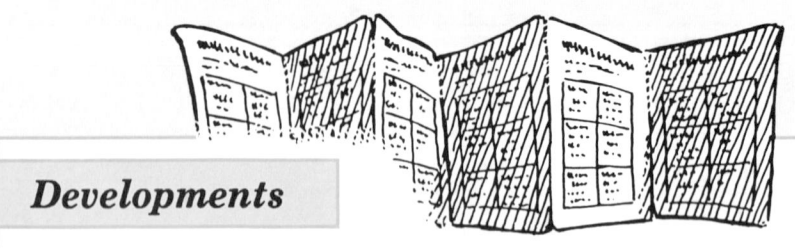

Developments

- Use the completed sheets as part of your record-keeping.
- Make a book of the sheets, for the children to browse through.
- Reflect on the children's responses. This can help to make a repeat of the project more successful.
- Make a display of some of the responses. Put the children's responses in speech bubbles, under the relevant headings.

What I thought about my project

My project's title: _____

Now that my project is finished ...

The best thing about the project was ...	What I want to remember most is ...
What still puzzles me is ...	Other areas of the project I'd like to explore are ...
The books that helped me most were ...	I think we did this project because ...

I talked about this sheet with _____.

Eight ways to help ...

There are hundreds of ideas in this book to enable you to develop and extend the photocopiable pages. Here are just eight ways to help you make the most of the Ideas Bank series.

1 Photocopy a page, paste on to card and laminate/cover with sticky-backed plastic to use with groups. Children can now write on the pages using water-based pens and this can be washed off.

2 Photocopy on to both sides of the paper. Put another useful activity on the back. Develop a simple filing system so others can find relevant sheets and do not duplicate them again.

3 Save the sheets - if the children do not have to cut them up as a part of the activity - and re-use. Label the sets, and keep them safely in files.

4 Make the most of group work. Children working in small groups need one sheet to discuss between them.

5 Put the sheets inside clear plastic wallets. This means the sheets are easily stored in a binder and will last longer. Children's writing can again be wiped away.

6 Use as an ideas page for yourself. Discuss issues with the class and get children to produce artwork and writing.

7 Make an overhead transparency of the page. You and your colleagues can now use the idea time and time again.

8 Ask yourself, 'Does every child in this class/group need to deal with/work through this photocopiable sheet?' If not, don't photocopy it!